Pebble® Plus

ICE AGE ANIMALS

Woolly Mammoths

by Melissa Higgins

Consulting Editor: Gail Saunders-Smith, PhD

Content Consultant: Margaret M. Yacobucci, PhD
Education and Outreach Coordinator,
Paleontological Society; Associate Professor,
Department of Geology, Bowling Green State University

Raintree is an imprint of Capstone Global Library Limited, a company incorporated in England and Wales having its registered office at 7 Pilgrim Street, London, EC4V 6LB – Registered company number: 6695582

www.raintree.co.uk
myorders@raintree.co.uk

Text © Capstone Global Library Limited 2015
The moral rights of the proprietor have been asserted.

Editorial Credits
Jeni Wittrock, editor; Peggie Carley and Janet Kusmierski, designers; Wanda Winch, media researcher; Laura Manthe, production specialist

ISBN 978 1 4062 9367 8 (hardback)
18 17 16 15 14
10 9 8 7 6 5 4 3 2 1

ISBN 978 1 4062 9374 6 (paperback)
19 18 17 16
10 9 8 7 6 5 4 3 2 1

British Library Cataloguing in Publication Data
A full catalogue record for this book is available from the British Library.

Photo Credits
Illustrator: Jon Hughes
Shutterstock: Alex Staroseltsev, snowball, April Cat, icicles, Kotkóa, cover background, Leigh Prather, ice crystals, pcruciatti, interior background

Contents

Ice-age giant

The ground shakes.

A 4-tonne woolly mammoth

lumbers over a hill. She leads

her herd to a green valley.

Mammoths lived during the
Ice Age. The climate was cool,
but there was plenty of grass.
Mammoths roamed in Europe,
Asia and North America.

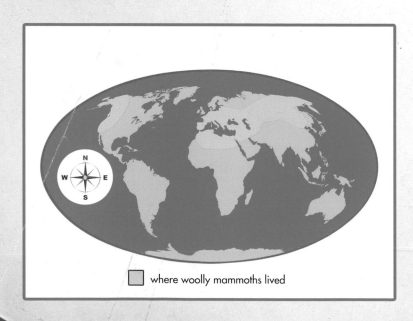

where woolly mammoths lived

Built for cold

A woolly mammoth was about the size of an elephant. But it was built for cold weather. Its small ears lost little heat. Long, shaggy fur kept it warm.

Tusks helped mammoths to dig up food buried in snow. Mothers used tusks to protect calves from predators. Males used tusks to fight with each other.

Happy grazing

Mammoths used their trunks to eat and drink. They ate mostly grass. They needed 227 kilograms (500 pounds) of food every day.

Two "fingers" on the tip of the
mammoth's trunk plucked grass.
Bumpy ridges on their teeth
ground these tough plants.

Mammoth life

Woolly mammoths lived in groups, like elephants today. One female would lead a herd of other females and calves. Adult males lived on their own.

Baby mammoths drank
their mothers' milk for up
to five years. Males stayed
with the herd until they
were young adults.

Over 10,000 years ago, the climate warmed. Mammoths could not find enough food. The last mammoths were killed by humans and other animals.

Glossary

calf baby woolly mammoth

climate average weather of a place throughout the year

grazer eats grass

herd group of mammoths

Ice Age time when much of Earth was covered in ice; the last ice age ended about 11,500 years ago

lumber walk with slow, heavy steps

predator animal that hunts other animals for food

protect keep safe

shaggy long and rough

trunk mammoth's long nose and upper lip

tusk pointed tooth that sticks out when the mouth is closed

Read more

First Encyclopedia of Dinosaurs and Prehistoric Life (Usborne First Encyclopedias), Sam Taplin (Usborne Publishing Ltd, 2011)

The Ice Age Tracker's Guide, Adrian Lister and Martin Ursell (Frances Lincoln Children's Books, 2010)

Woolly Mammoth, Mick Manning and Brita Granstrom (Frances Lincoln Children's Books, 2011)

Websites

www.bbc.co.uk/nature/life/Woolly_mammoth
Learn more about the woolly mammoth and follow the links to find out how they managed to survive the extreme cold of the Ice Age!

www.nhm.ac.uk/kids-only/dinosaurs/
Find out everything you need to know about prehistoric life. Look at 3-D dinosaurs, learn fun facts, play games and take a quiz!

Index